The Chinese Revolution and the Theses of Comrade Stalin

# The Chinese Revolution and the Theses of Comrade Stalin

## Problems of the Chinese Revolution

By

Leon Trotsky

Aspekt Publishers

The Chinese Revolution and the Theses of Comrade Stalin

© Leon Trotsky
© 2022 Uitgeverij ASPEKT / Aspekt Publishers
Amersfoortsestraat 27, 3769 AD Soesterberg, The Netherlands
info@uitgeverijaspekt.nl – http://www.uitgeverijaspekt.nl

Cover: Snegina Uzunova
Inside: Sjoerd van 't Slot

ISBN: 9789464620023
NUR: 680

All rights reserved. No reproduction copy or transmission of this publication may be made without written permission.

# May 17, 1927

The theses of comrade Stalin entitled *Problems of the Chinese Revolution* were published in **Pravda** on April 21, 1927, a few days after the close of the plenary session of the Central Committee, to which these theses were never presented and at which they were never discussed (although all the members of the plenum were still in Moscow).

Moreover, the theses of comrade Stalin are erroneous to such a point, they turn the matter upside down to such a degree, they are so permeated with the spirit of *chvostism*, they are so inclined to perpetuate the mistakes already made, that to remain silent about them would be a positive crime.

# The Lessons of the Chinese Events Must Be Drawn

1) The prohibition of an open discussion of the theoretical and tactical problems of the Chinese revolution has been motivated of late by the fact that such a discussion would delight the enemies of the USSR. Naturally it would be quite impermissible to make public facts that could be seized upon by enemies, who, incidentally, do not shrink from the direct invention of "facts" and "documents". But there is no need at all for such a discussion. It is only a question of determining the driving forces of the Chinese revolution and of estimating the basic line of its political direction. In other words, it is a question of discussing *the same questions to which the theses of comrade Stalin are devoted*. If these theses can be published, then why cannot a criticism of them be published?

It is an unheard-of mistake to contend that a discussion of the problems of the Chinese revolution can injure our state interests. If this were so, then not only the Communist Party of the Soviet Union but every other party of the Communist International, including the Chinese, would have to abstain from any discussion. But the interests of the Chinese revolution, as well as the interests of the education of all the Communist parties in the world, demand an open, energetic, exhaustive discussion of all the problems of the Chinese revolution, especially those in dispute. It is not true that the interests of the Communist International conflict with the state interests of the USSR. The renunciation of discussion of the mistakes is not dictated by the interests of a workers' state, but by a false "apparatus-like", bureaucratic attitude towards the Chinese revolution as well as towards the interests of the USSR.

2) The April defeat of the Chinese revolution is not only a defeat for the opportunist line but also a defeat for the bureaucratic methods of the leadership, through which the Party is confronted with every decision as an accomplished fact: the decision, it is explained, does not justify criticism until facts demonstrate its annulment, whereupon it is just as automatically, that is, behind the back of the Party, replaced by a decision which is frequently more erroneous, like the present theses of Stalin. Such a method, which, in and by itself, is incompatible with the development of a revolutionary party, becomes an especially heavy obstacle to young parties that can and should learn independently from the experiences of defeats and mistakes.

The theses of comrade Stalin are published. At least within the limits of these theses, the questions of the Chinese revolution can and must be discussed openly and from every angle.

# The Yoke of Imperialism and the Class Struggle

3) The peculiarity of the Chinese revolution – in comparison, for example, with our revolution of 1905 – lies above all in the semi-colonial position in China. A policy that disregarded the powerful pressure of imperialism on the internal life of China would be radically false. But a policy that proceeded from an abstract conception of national oppression without its class refraction and reflection would be no less false. The main source of the mistakes in the theses of comrade Stalin, as in the whole leading line in general, is the false conception of the role of imperialism and its influence on the class relationships of China.

The imperialist yoke is supposed to serve as a justification for the policy of the "bloc of four classes". The yoke of imperialism leads allegedly to the fact that "all" the classes of China look upon the Canton government as the "national government of the whole of China in the same way". (Speech of comrade Kalinin, **Izvestia**, March 6) This is essentially the position of the right Guomindang man, Dai Tshi Tao, who pretends that the laws of the class struggle do not exist for China – because of imperialist pressure.

China is an oppressed semi-colonial country. The development of the productive forces of China, which is proceeding in capitalist forms, demands the shaking off of the imperialist yoke. The war of China for its national independence is a progressive war, because it flows from the necessities of the economic and cultural development of China itself, as well as because it facilitates the development of the revolution of the British proletariat and that of the whole world proletariat.

But this by no means signifies that the imperialist yoke is a mechanical one, subjugating "all" the classes of China in the "same" way. The powerful role of foreign capital in the life of China has caused very strong sections of the Chinese bourgeoisie, the bureaucracy and the military to join their destiny with that of imperialism. Without this tie, the enormous role of the so-called "militarists" in the life of modern China would be inconceivable.

It would further be profound *naïveté* to believe that an abyss lies between the so-called comprador bourgeoisie, that is, the economic and political agency of foreign capital in China, and the so-called "national" bourgeoisie. No, these two sections stand incomparably closer to each other than the bourgeoisie and the masses of workers and peasants. The bourgeoisie participated in the national war as an internal brake, looking upon the worker and peasant masses with growing hostility, and becoming ever readier to conclude a compromise with imperialism.

Installed within the Guomindang and its leadership, the national bourgeoisie has been essentially an instrument of the compradors and imperialism. It can remain in the camp of the national war only because of the weakness of the worker and peasant masses, the lack of development of the class struggle, the lack of independence of the Chinese Communist Party and the docility of the Guomindang in the hands of the bourgeoisie.

It is a gross mistake to think that imperialism mechanically welds together all the classes of China from without. That is the position of the Chinese Kadet, Dai Tshi Tao, but in no wise ours. The revolutionary struggle against imperialism does not weaken, but rather strengthens the political differentiation of the classes. Imperialism is a highly powerful force in the internal relationships of China. The main source of this force is not the warships in the waters of the Yangtze Kiang – they are only auxiliaries – but the economic and political bond between foreign capital and the native bourgeoisie. The struggle against imperialism, precisely because of its economic and military power, demands a powerful exertion of forces from the very depths of the Chinese people. To really arouse the workers and peasants against imperialism is possible only by connecting their basic and most profound life interests with the cause of the country's liberation. A workers' strike – small or large – an agrarian rebellion, an uprising of the oppressed sections in city and country against the usurer, against the bureaucracy, against the local military satraps, all that arouses the multitudes, that welds them together, that educates, steels, is a real step forward on the road to the revolutionary and social liberation of the Chinese people. Without that, the military successes and failures of the right, semi-right or semi-left generals will remain foam on the surface of the ocean. But everything that brings the oppressed and exploited masses of the toilers to their feet inevitably pushes the national bourgeoisie into an open bloc with the imperialists. The class struggle between the bourgeoisie and the masses of workers and peasants is not weakened, but, on the contrary, is sharpened by imperialist oppression, to the point of bloody civil war at every serious conflict. The Chinese bourgeoisie always has a solid rearguard behind it in imperialism, which will always help it with money, goods and shells against the workers and peasants.

Only wretched philistines and sycophants, who hope in their hearts to obtain freedom for China as an imperialist bounty for the good behaviour of the masses, can believe that the national liberation of China can be achieved by moderating the class struggle, by curbing strikes and agrarian uprisings, by abandoning the arming of the masses, etc. When comrade Martynov proposes that strikes and the struggle on the land be replaced by a solution of the questions through the medium of governmental arbitration, then he differs in no way from Dai Tshi Tao, the philosophical inspirer of Chiang Kai-shek's policy.

# Democratic or Socialist Revolution?

4) The senseless contention is attributed to the Opposition that China now stands on the eve of a socialist dictatorship of the proletariat. There is nothing original in this "criticism". On the eve of 1905 and later on, the Mensheviks frequently declared that Lenin's tactic would be correct if Russia were directly on the eve of the socialist revolution. Lenin, however, explained to them that his tactic was the only road to the radical victory of the democratic revolution which, under favourable conditions, would begin to grow over into a socialist revolution.

The question of the "non-capitalist" path of development of China was posed in a conditional form by Lenin, for whom, as for us, it was and is ABC wisdom that the Chinese revolution, left to its own forces, that is, *without the direct support of the victorious proletariat of the USSR and the working class of all advanced countries*, could end only with the conquest of the broadest possibilities for the capitalist development of the country, with more favourable conditions for the labour movement.

5) No less basically false is the contention that the question as to whether the Chinese proletariat needs an independent party; whether this party needs a bloc with the Guomindang or must subordinate itself to it; whether soviets are necessary, etc., must be solved in accordance with how we conceive the course and the tempo of the *further* stages of the Chinese revolution.

It is quite possible that China will have to pass through a relatively prolonged stage of parliamentarism, beginning with a Constituent Assembly. This demand is inscribed on the banner of the Communist Party. If the bourgeois democratic revolution does not grow into a socialist revolution in the near future, then in all probability the workers' and peasants' soviets will pass from the scene for a definite stage and give way to a bourgeois régime, which, depending on the progress of the world revolution, will in turn give way, at a new historical stage, to the dictatorship of the proletariat.

6) But first of all, the inevitability of the capitalist path has by no means been proved; and secondly – this argument is now incomparably more timely for us – the bourgeois tasks can be solved in various ways. The slogan of the Constituent Assembly becomes an empty abstraction, often simple charlatanry, if one does not add who will convoke it and with what program. Chiang Kai-shek can raise the slogan of a Constituent Assembly against us even tomorrow, just as he has now raised his "workers' and peasants' program" against us. We want a Constituent Assembly convoked not by Chiang Kai-shek but by the executive committee of the workers' and peasants' soviets. That is the only serious and sure road.

7) Basically untenable is the endeavour of comrade Bukharin to justify the opportunist and compromising line by referring to the allegedly predominant role of the "remnants of feudalism" in Chinese economy. Even if comrade Bukharin's estimation of Chinese economy rested on an economic analysis and not on scholastic

definitions, the "remnants of feudalism" would still be unable to justify the policy which so manifestly facilitated the April *coup d'état*.

The Chinese revolution has a national bourgeois character principally because the development of the productive forces of Chinese capitalism collides with its governmental customs dependence upon the countries of imperialism. The obstruction of the development of Chinese industry and the throttling of the internal market involve the conservation and rebirth of the most backward forms of production in agriculture, of the most parasitic forms of exploitation, of the most barbaric forms of oppression and violence, the growth of surplus population, as well as the persistence and aggravation of pauperism and all sorts of slavery. No matter how great the specific weight of the typically "feudal" elements in Chinese economy may be they can be swept away only in a revolutionary way, and consequently not in alliance with the bourgeoisie but in direct struggle against it. The more complicated and tortuous is the interlacing of feudal and capitalist relations, the less the agrarian question can be solved by legislation from above, the more indispensable is the revolutionary initiative of the peasant masses in close union with the workers and the poor population of the cities, the falser is the policy that clings convulsively to the alliance with the bourgeoisie and the large landowner and subordinates its work among the masses to this alliance. The policy of the "bloc of four classes" not only prepared the bloc of the bourgeoisie with imperialism, but also meant the preservation of all the survivals of barbarism in administration and in economy.

To invoke the bourgeois character of the Chinese revolution, in particular against the soviets, is simply to renounce the experiences of our bourgeois revolutions of 1905 and February 1917. In these revolutions, the immediate and essential objective was the abolition of the autocratic and feudal régime. This aim did not exclude, but demanded the arming of the workers and the formation of soviets. Here is how Lenin treated the subject after the February revolution:

> "For an effective struggle against the tsarist monarchy, for a real assurance of liberty not only in words, not in elegant promises of the rhetoricians of liberalism, the workers must *not* support the new government, but the government must 'support' the workers. For the only *guarantee* of freedom and of the final destruction of tsarism is *the arming of the proletariat*, the consolidation, the extension, the development of the role, the significance, and the power of the workers' and soldiers' soviets. Everything else is phrases and lies of the politicians in the liberal and radical camps who are deceiving themselves. Support the arming of the workers or at least do not obstruct this process, and freedom in Russia will be invincible, the monarchy irretrievable, the republic assured. Otherwise the people will be deceived. Promises are cheap. They cost nothing. All the bourgeois politicians in *all* the bourgeois revolutions have 'fed' the people with promises and stupefied the workers. Our revolution is a bourgeois revolution, *therefore* the workers must support the bourgeoisie; that is what the worthless politicians from the camp of the liquidators say. Our revolution is a bourgeois

revolution, say we, the Marxists; therefore the workers must open the eyes of the people to the deception of the bourgeois politicians, must teach it to put no trust in words, to rely upon *its own* forces, *its own* organization, *its own* unity, *its own* arms."

The Chinese revolutionist who casts the over-cunning resolutions and comments on the bloc of four classes out of his head, will firmly grasp the sense of these simple words of Lenin, will be sure not to go astray and will attain the goal.

# The School of Martynov in the Chinese Question

8) The official leadership of the Chinese revolution has been oriented all this time on a "general national united front" or on the "bloc of four classes" (cf. the report of Bukharin; the leader in **Communist International**, no.11; the unpublished speech by Stalin to the Moscow functionaries on April 5, 1927; the article by Martynov in **Pravda** on April 10; the leader in **Pravda** of March 16; the speech by comrade Kalinin in **Izvestia** of March 6, 1927; the speech by comrade Rudzutak in **Pravda** of March 9, 1927; etc., etc.). Matters had gone so far on this track, that on the eve of Chiang Kai-shek's *coup d'état*, **Pravda**, in order to expose the Opposition, proclaimed that revolutionary China was not being ruled by a bourgeois government but by a "government of the bloc of four classes".

The philosophy of Martynov, which has the sorry courage to carry all the mistakes of Stalin and Bukharin in the questions of Chinese policy to their logical conclusion, does not meet a trace of objection. Yet it is tantamount to trampling under foot the fundamental principles of Marxism. It reproduces the crudest features of Russian and international Menshevism, applied to the conditions of the Chinese revolution. Not for nothing does the present leader of the Mensheviks, Dan, write in the last number of **Sotsialisticheski Vestnik:**

> "'In principle' the Bolsheviks were also for retaining the 'united front' in the Chinese revolution up

to the completion of the task of national liberation. On April 10, Martynov, in **Pravda**, most effectively and despite the obligatory abuse of the Social Democrats, in a quite 'Menshevik manner' showed the 'Left' Oppositionist Radek the correctness of the *official* position which insists on the necessity of retaining the 'bloc of four classes', on not hastening to overthrow the coalition government in which the workers sit side by side with the big bourgeoisie, not to impose 'socialist tasks' upon it prematurely."

Everyone who knows the history of the struggle of Bolshevism against Menshevism, particularly in the question of relations to the liberal bourgeoisie, must acknowledge that Dan's approval of the "rational principles" of the Martynov school is not accidental, but follows with perfect legitimacy. It is only unnatural that this school should raise its voice with impunity in the ranks of the Comintern.

The old Menshevik tactic of 1905 to 1917, which was crushed under foot by the march of events, is now transferred to China by the Martynov school, much the same as capitalist trade dumps its most inferior merchandise, which finds no market in the mother country, into the colonies. The merchandise has not even been renovated. The arguments are the same, letter for letter, as they were twenty years ago. Only, where formerly the word *autocracy* stood, the word *imperialism* has been substituted for it in the text. Naturally, British imperialism is different from autocracy. But the Menshevik reference to it does not differ in the slightest from its reference to autocracy. The struggle against foreign imperialism is as much a class struggle as the struggle against autocracy. That it cannot be exorcized by the idea of the national united front, is far too eloquently proved by the bloody April events, a direct consequence of the policy of the bloc of four classes.

# What the "Line" Looked Like in Practice

9) On the past period, which terminated with the April *coup d'état*, the theses of comrade Stalin announce:

> "The line adopted was the only correct line."

What did it look like in practice? An eloquent reply is supplied by Tang Pingshan, the Communist minister of agriculture, in his report at the Seventh Plenum of the ECCI in December 1926.

> "Since the establishment of the national government in Canton last July, which is nominally a government of the left wing, *the power has actually been in the hands of the right wing* ... The movement of the workers and peasants cannot develop to its full breadth as a result of various obstacles. After the March putsch a *military dictatorship of the centre* [that is, Chiang Kai-shek] was established, while the political power remained as before in the hands of the right wing. The whole political power, which should properly have belonged to the left wing, is finally lost."

So: the left "should have" had the power, but finally lost it; the state power belonged to the right, the military authority, which is incomparably more powerful, arid was entirely in the hands of the "centre" of Chiang Kai-shek, which became the centre of the conspiracy. Under such conditions, it is not difficult to understand why "the movement of the workers and peasants" could not develop as it should have.

Tang Pingshan gives an even more precise characterization of what the "only correct line" looked like in reality:

> "... We sacrificed the interests of the workers and peasants in practice ... After lengthy negotiations with us, the government did not as much as promulgate a trade-union law ... The government did not accept the demands of the peasantry, which we presented to it in the name of various social organizations. When conflicts arose between the large landowners and the poor peasants, the government always took the side of the former."

How could all this happen? Tang Pingshan cautiously names two reasons:

a) "The left leaders are not capable of consolidating and extending their influence by means of political power";

b) The right wing "won the possibility to act, partly *as a result of our wrong tactic*".

10) Such are, the political relations that received the pompous title of the "bloc of four classes". Such "blocs" abound in the revolutionary as well as the parliamentary history of bourgeois countries: the big bourgeoisie leads the petty-bourgeois democrats, the phrase-mongers of the national united front, behind it, and the latter, in turn, confuse the workers and drag them along

behind the bourgeoisie. When the proletarian "tail", despite the efforts of the petty-bourgeois phrase-mongers, begins to stir too violently, the bourgeoisie orders its generals to stamp on it. Then the opportunists observe with an air of profundity that the bourgeoisie has "betrayed" the national cause.

11) But did not the Chinese bourgeoisie "nevertheless" fight against imperialism? This argument too is an empty commonplace. The compromisers of every country, in similar cases, have always assured the workers that the liberal bourgeoisie is fighting against reaction. The Chinese bourgeoisie utilized the petty-bourgeois democracy only in order to conclude an alliance with imperialism against the workers. The Northern expedition only served to strengthen the bourgeoisie and weaken the workers. A tactic that prepared such a result is a false tactic. "We sacrificed the interests of the workers and peasants in practice," says Tang Pingshan. What for? To support the bloc of four classes. And the results? A colossal success of the bourgeois counter-revolution, the consolidation of shattered imperialism, the weakening of the USSR. Such a policy is criminal. Unless it is mercilessly condemned, we cannot take a step forward.

## The Theses Justify a Line for Which There Is No Justification

12) The theses endeavour even now to justify the policy which united the party of the proletariat with the big bourgeoisie within the framework of one organization, the Guomindang, where the whole leadership was in the hands of the bourgeoisie. The theses declare: "This was the line ... for the utilization of the rights, their connections and experiences, in so far as they submitted to the discipline of the Guomindang." Now we know very well how the bourgeoisie submitted to "discipline" and how the proletariat utilized the rights, that is, the big and middle bourgeoisie, their "connections" (with the imperialists) and their "experiences" (in strangling and shooting the workers). The story of this "utilization" is written in the book of the Chinese revolution with letters of blood. But this does not prevent the theses from saying: "The subsequent events fully confirmed the correctness of this line." Further than this no one can go!

From an enormous counter-revolutionary *coup d'état*, the theses of Stalin draw the positively miserable conclusion that the policy of "isolating the right" within the united Guomindang must be "replaced" by a policy of "determined struggle" against the right. All this after the right-wing "comrades" have begun to speak in the language of machine-guns.

13) The theses refer, to be sure, to a "previous prediction" on the inevitability of the bourgeoisie's withdrawal from the revolution. But are such prophecies

by themselves sufficient for a Bolshevik policy? The prediction that the bourgeoisie will quit is an empty commonplace unless definite political conclusions are drawn from it. In the already quoted article, which approves the semi-official line of Martynov, Dan writes: "In a movement that embraces such antagonistic classes, *the united front cannot of course last forever.*"

So Dan also acknowledges the "inevitability of the bourgeoisie's withdrawal". In practice, however, the policy of Menshevism in the revolution consists of retaining the united front at any cost, as long as possible, at the price of adapting its own policy to the policy of the bourgeoisie, at the price of cutting down the slogans and the activity of the masses, and even, as in China, at the price of the organizational subordination of the workers' party to the political apparatus of the bourgeoisie. The Bolshevik way, however, consists of an unconditional political and organizational demarcation from the bourgeoisie, of a relentless exposure of the bourgeoisie from the very first steps of the revolution, of a destruction of all petty-bourgeois illusions about the united front with the bourgeoisie, of tireless struggle with the bourgeoisie for the leadership of the masses, of the merciless expulsion from the Communist Party of all those elements who sow vain hopes in the bourgeoisie or idealize them.

# Two Paths and the Mistakes of the Past

14) The theses of comrade Stalin, to be sure, seek to oppose to each other the two paths of development of the Chinese revolution: one under the leadership of the bourgeoisie, with its suppression of the proletariat and an inevitable alliance with foreign imperialism; the other under the leadership of the proletariat against the bourgeoisie.

But in order that this second prospect of the bourgeois-democratic revolution should not remain an empty phrase, it must be said openly and plainly that the whole leadership of the Chinese revolution up to now has been in irreconcilable contradiction to it. The Opposition has been and is subjected to a rabid criticism precisely because, from the very beginning, it brought to the fore the Leninist manner of putting the question, that is, the path of the struggle of the proletariat against the bourgeoisie for the leadership of the oppressed masses of city and country within the framework and on the foundation of the national-democratic revolution.

15) From the theses of Stalin it follows that the proletariat can separate itself from the bourgeoisie only after the latter has tossed it aside, disarmed it, beheaded it and crushed it under foot. But this is precisely the way the abortive revolution of 1848 developed, where the proletariat had no banner of its own, but followed at the heels of the petty-bourgeois democracy, which in turn trotted behind the liberal bourgeoisie and led the

workers under the sabre of Cavaignac. Great though the real peculiarities of the Chinese situation may be, the fundamentals that characterized the development of the 1848 revolution have been repeated in the Chinese revolution with such deadly precision as though neither the lessons of 1848, 1871, 1905 and 1917 nor those of the Communist Party of the Soviet Union and the Comintern had ever existed.

That Chiang Kai-shek played the role of a republican-liberal Cavaignac has already become a commonplace. The theses of Stalin, following the Opposition, recognize this analogy. But the analogy must be supplemented. Cavaignac would have been impossible without the Ledru-Rollins, the Louis Blancs and the other phrasemongers of the all-inclusive national front. And who played these roles in China? Not only Wang Jingwei, but also the leaders of the Chinese Communist Party, above all their inspirers of the ECCI. Unless this is stated openly, explained and deeply impressed, the philosophy of – the two paths of development will only serve to screen opportunism *à la* Louis Blanc and Martynov, that is, to prepare a repetition of the April tragedy at a new stage of the Chinese revolution.

# The Position of the Chinese Communist Party

16) In order to have the right to speak about the struggle for the Bolshevik path of the democratic revolution, one must possess the principal instrument of proletarian policy; *an independent proletarian party* which fights under its own banner and never permits its policy and organization to be dissolved in the policy and organization of other classes. Without assuring the complete theoretical, political and organizational independence of the Communist Party, all talk about "two paths" is a mockery of Bolshevism. The Chinese Communist Party, in this whole period, has not been *in alliance* with the revolutionary petty-bourgeois section of the Guomindang, but *in subordination* to the whole Guomindang, led in reality by the bourgeoisie which had the army and the power in its hands. The Communist Party submitted to the political discipline of Chiang Kai-shek. The Communist Party signed the obligation not to criticize Sun-Yat-Sen-ism, a petty-bourgeois theory which is directed not only against imperialism, but also against the class struggle. The Communist Party did not have its own press, that is, it lacked the principal weapon of an independent party. Under such conditions, to speak of the struggle of the proletariat for hegemony means to deceive oneself and others.

17) By what is the submissive, indistinct, and politically unworthy position of the Communist Party in Chiang Kai-shek's Guomindang to be explained? By the insistence upon the unity of the national front under the

actual leadership of the bourgeoisie which allegedly "could not" withdraw from the revolution (the school of Martynov), that is, the rejection in practice of the second, Bolshevik path of which the theses of Stalin speak as an afterthought, solely for camouflage purposes.

To justify such a policy by the necessity for an alliance of the workers and peasants, is to reduce this alliance itself to a phrase, to a screen for the commanding role of the bourgeoisie. The dependence of the Communist Party, an inevitable result of the "bloc of the four classes", was the main obstacle in the path of the workers' and peasants' movement, and therefore also of the real alliance between the proletariat and the peasantry, without which the victory of the Chinese revolution cannot even be thought of.

18) What should the Communist Party do in the future?

In the theses, there is only a single sentence on this, but one capable of sowing the greatest confusion and causing irreparable harm. "... While fighting in the ranks of the revolutionary Guomindang," say Stalin's theses, "the Communist Party must *preserve its independence* more than ever before." Preserve? But to this day the Communist Party has had no such independence. Precisely its lack of independence is the source of all the evils and all the mistakes. In this fundamental question, the theses, instead of making an end once and for all to the practice of yesterday, propose to retain it "more than ever before". But this means that they want to retain the ideological, political and organizational dependence of the proletarian party upon a petty-bourgeois party, which is inevitably converted into an instrument of the big bourgeoisie.

In order to justify a false policy, one is forced to call dependence independence, and to demand the preservation of what ought to be buried for all time.

19) Chinese Bolshevism can rise only under a merciless self-criticism by the best elements of the Communist Party. To support them in this is our direct duty. The attempt to cover up the mistakes of the past by artificially curbing a discussion of them, will cause enormous harm, primarily to the Chinese Communist Party. If we do not help it to purge itself, in the shortest period, from Menshevism and the Mensheviks, it will enter a prolonged crisis, with splits, desertions, and an embittered struggle of various groups. What is more, the heavy defeats of opportunism may clear a road to anarcho-syndicalist influences.

If, in spite of a workers' mass movement, in spite of the powerful rise of the trade unions, in spite of the revolutionary agrarian movement on the land, the Communist Party should remain as before an integral appendage to a bourgeois party, and what is more, should it enter the national government created by this bourgeois party, it would be better to say frankly: the time has not yet come for a Communist party in China. It is better not to constitute any Communist party at all than to discredit it so cruelly at the time of a revolution, that is, just at the time when the Party is being joined to the working masses with bonds of blood and when great traditions are being created that are destined to live for decades.

# Who Was Mistaken on the Tempo?

20) In Stalin's theses there is of course a whole section devoted to the "mistakes of the Opposition". Instead of hitting out at the right, that is, at the mistakes of Stalin himself, the theses are intent upon striking at the left, thereby deepening the mistakes, piling up confusion, making the way out more difficult, and driving the line of the leadership down into the swamp of compromise.

21) The main accusation: the Opposition "does not understand that the revolution in China cannot develop at a rapid tempo". For some reason or other, the theses drag in here the tempo of the October revolution. If the question of tempo is raised, it must not be measured with the external yardstick of the October revolution, but with the internal class relationships of the Chinese revolution itself. The Chinese bourgeoisie, as is known, paid no attention to the precepts about a slow tempo. In April 1927, it considered it quite opportune to throw off the mask of the united front which had served it so well, in order to open an attack upon the revolution with all its strength. The Communist Party, the proletariat, as well as the Left Guomindang people, showed themselves completely unprepared for this blow. Why? Because the leadership counted upon a slower tempo, because it remained hopelessly behindhand, because it was infected with *chvostism*.

On April 23, that is, after the *coup d'état* by Chiang Kai-shek, the Central Committee of the Guomindang, together with the "left" Wuhan government, published a manifesto, which said:

> *"It only remains for us to regret [!] that we did not act when there was still time. For that we apologize sincerely."*

In these doleful and whining avowals lies, against the will of their authors, a pitiless refutation of the Stalinist philosophy on the "tempo" of the Chinese revolution.

22) We continued to maintain the bloc with the bourgeoisie at a time when the working masses were driving towards independent struggle. We attempted to utilize the experiences of the "rights" and became playthings in their hands. We carried on an ostrich policy in the press, by suppressing and concealing from our own party the first *coup d'état* by Chiang Kai-shek in March 1926, the shootings of workers and peasants, and in general all the facts that marked the counter-revolutionary character of the Guomindang leadership. We neglected to look after the independence of our own party. We founded no newspaper for it. "We sacrificed the interests of the workers and peasants in practice" (Tang Pingshan). We did not take a single serious step to win over the soldiers. We allowed the Chiang Kai-shek band to establish a "military dictatorship of the centre", that is, a dictatorship of the bourgeois counter-revolution. On the very eve of the *coup d'état* we blew the trumpets for Chiang Kai-shek. We declared that he had "submitted to discipline", and that we had succeeded "by a skilful tactical manoeuvre in forestalling an abrupt turn to the right that threatened the

Chinese revolution". We remained behind the events all along the line. At every step we lost in tempo to the benefit of the bourgeoisie. In this way we prepared the most favourable conditions for the bourgeois counter-revolution. The Left Guomindang at least offers us its "sincere apology". The theses of Stalin, on the contrary, draw from this whole chain of truly unparalleled chvostist mistakes the remarkable conclusion that the Opposition demands. a too rapid tempo.

23) Ever more frequently one hears accusations at our party meetings against the "ultra-left" Shanghaiers and in general against the Chinese workers for having provoked Chiang Kai-shek by their "excesses". No one cites any examples; and what would they prove, anyway? Not a single real people's revolution, drawing millions into its vortex, proceeds without so-called "excesses". A policy which seeks to prescribe for the masses just awakening a line of march that will not disturb the bourgeois "order" is a policy of incurable philistines. It will always break its head against the logic of civil war when, while pronouncing belated curses upon the Cavaignacs and Kornilovs, it denounces at the same time the alleged "excesses" of the left.

The "mistake" of the Chinese workers lies in the fact that the critical moment of the revolution found them unprepared, unorganized and unarmed. But that is not their mistake, it is their misfortune. The responsibility for it falls entirely upon a bad leadership, which let every interval pass.

# Does a New Revolutionary Centre Already Exist or Must One First Be Created?

24) On the present state of the Chinese revolution, the theses proclaim: "Chiang Kai-shek's *coup d'état* means that there will now be two camps, two governments, two armies, two centres in the South: a revolutionary centre in Wuhan and a counter-revolutionary centre in Nanking." What an inexact, superficial, vulgar characterization! It is not simply a question of two halves of the Guomindang but of a new grouping of class forces. To believe that the Wuhan government is already a finished centre, which will simply continue the revolution from the point where it was brought to a stop and beaten to the ground by Chiang Kai-shek, is to regard the counter-revolutionary *coup d'état* in April as a personal "desertion", an "episode"; in a word, it is to understand nothing.

The workers were not simply crushed. They were crushed by those who led them. Can one believe that the masses will now follow the Left Guomindang with the same confidence that they accorded the whole Guomindang yesterday? From now on the struggle must be conducted not only against the former militarists allied with imperialism, but also against the "national" bourgeoisie which, as a result of our radically incorrect policy, has captured the military apparatus and considerable sections of the army.

For the struggle on a new, higher stage of the revolution, the deceived masses must above all be inspired with confidence in themselves, and the not yet awakened masses must be aroused. For this, it must first of all be demonstrated that not a trace has been left of that disgraceful policy which "sacrificed the interests of the workers and peasants" (cf. Tang Pingshan) in order to support the bloc of the four classes. Anyone who will lean in the direction of this policy must be mercilessly driven out of the Chinese Communist Party.

The miserably superficial and bureaucratic idea must be thrown aside that now, after the sanguinary experiences, millions of workers and peasants can be set in motion and led if only the "banner" of the Guomindang is waved around in the air a little. (We will surrender the blue banner of the Guomindang to nobody! cries Bukharin.)

No, the masses need a revolutionary program and a fighting organization which grows out of their own ranks and contains within itself the guarantee of contact with the masses and of loyalty to them. The Wuhan authorities are not enough for this: workers', peasants' and soldiers' soviets are needed for this, soviets of the toilers.

## Soviets and the Arming of the Workers and Peasants

25) After rejecting the vital and indispensable slogan of soviets, the theses of comrade Stalin declare somewhat unexpectedly that the principal "antidote to the counter-revolution is the arming of the workers and peasants". The arming of the workers is undoubtedly a necessary thing. We will have no differences at all on this point. But how are we to explain why it was considered correct up to now to arm the workers to a "minimum" extent for the welfare of the revolution? that the representatives of the Comintern actually *opposed* the arming of the workers? (cf. the letter of the four comrades to the delegation of the CPSU in the Comintern); that in spite of the full possibility of arming themselves the workers found themselves unarmed at the moment of the *coup d'état?* All this is to be explained by the desire not to break with Chiang Kai-shek, not to offend Chiang Kai-shek, not to push him to the right. The marvellous "antidote" was lacking precisely on the day when it was most needed. Today the workers are not arming themselves in Wuhan either – so as "not to drive away" Wang Jingwei.

26) The arming of the workers and peasants is an excellent thing. But one must be logical. In Southern China there are already armed peasants; they are the so-called National armies. Yet, far from being an "antidote to the counter-revolution", they have been its tool. Why? Because the political leadership, instead of embracing the masses of the army through soldiers' soviets has

contented itself with a purely external copy of our political departments and commissars, which, without an independent revolutionary party and without soldiers' soviets, have been transformed into an empty camouflage for bourgeois militarism.

27) The theses of Stalin reject the slogan of soviets with the argument that it would be a "slogan of struggle against the government of the revolutionary Guomindang". But in that case, what is the meaning of the words: "The principal antidote to the counter-revolution is the arming of the workers and peasants"? Against whom will the workers and peasants arm themselves? Will it not be against the governmental authority of the revolutionary Guomindang?

The slogan of arming the workers and peasants, if it is not a phrase, a subterfuge, a masquerade, but a call to action, is not less sharp in character than the slogan of workers' and peasants' soviets. Is it likely that the armed masses will tolerate at their side or over them the governmental authority of a bureaucracy alien and hostile to them? The real arming of the workers and peasants under present circumstances inevitably involves the formation of soviets.

28) Further: Who will arm the masses? Who will direct the armed men?

So long as the national armies marched forward and the Northern armies yielded ground, the arming of the workers could proceed with relative ease. The timely organization of workers', peasants' and soldiers' soviets would have meant a real "antidote" to the counter-revolution. Unfortunately, the mistakes of the past are irreparable. The whole situation has now taken a sharp turn for the worse. The few weapons seized spontaneously by the workers (are not these the "excesses" that are spoken of?) have been torn from them. The advance to the North has been suspended. Under these conditions the arming of the workers and peasants is a labourious and difficult task. To declare that the time for the soviets has not yet arrived and at the same time to launch the slogan for arming the workers and peasants, is to sow confusion. Only the soviets, at a further development of the revolution, can become the organs capable of really conducting the arming of the workers and of directing these armed masses.

# Why Is It Impossible to Form Soviets?

29) To this, the theses reply: "In the first place soviets cannot be created at any convenient moment, they are created only in the period of a special rise of the revolutionary wave." If these words have any sense at all, it is this: We let pass the favourable moment when we did not call upon the masses to create soviets at the beginning of the last period of powerful revolutionary rise. Once again: the mistakes of the past are irreparable. If we are of the opinion that the Chinese revolution has been crushed for a long time, then the slogan of soviets will naturally find no echo in the masses. But all the more unfounded then is the slogan of the arming of the workers and peasants. We do not believe, however, that the consequences of the false policy pursued are so heavy and profound. There are many facts that speak for the possibility and the likelihood of a new revolutionary rise in the near future. Among other things, it is indicated by the fact that Chiang Kai-shek is forced to flirt with the masses, to promise the workers the eight-hour day, and all sorts of relief to the peasants, etc. In the event of a further extension of the agrarian movement and a turning of the petty-bourgeois masses of the city against Chiang Kai-shek as an open agent of imperialism, more favourable conditions can arise in the near future under which the now battered proletarian vanguard will reassemble the ranks of the toilers for a new offensive. Whether this will take place a month sooner or later is of no concern; in any case we must prepare for it now with our own program and our own

organizations. In other words: *the slogan of soviets will henceforth accompany the whole further course of the Chinese revolution and reflect its destinies.*

30) "In the second place," say the theses, "soviets are not formed for chattering; they are created primarily as organs of struggle against the existing state power, and for the conquest of power." That soviets are not created for chattering is perhaps the only correct point in the theses. But a revolutionist does not propose the arming of the workers and peasants for chattering either. Whoever says here: at the present stage only chatter can be the result of soviets, but on the contrary, something serious will come out of the arming of the workers and peasants, is either making fun of himself or of others.

31) A third argument: since there is now a series of Left Guomindang organizations in Wuhan, which in their solemn manifesto of April 23 apologized for having overslept the *coup d'état* of Chiang Kai-shek, the theses draw the conclusion: the creation of soviets would mean an insurrection against the Left Guomindang, "for there is no other governmental authority in this region at present than that of the revolutionary Guomindang".

These words fairly reek with the apparatus-like, bureaucratic conception of revolutionary authority. The government is not regarded as the expression and consolidation of the developing struggle of the classes, but as the self-sufficient expression of the will of the Guomindang. The classes come and go but the continuity of the Guomindang goes on for ever. But it is not enough to call Wuhan the centre of the revolution for it really to be that. The provincial Guomindang of Chiang Kai-shek had an old, reactionary, mercenary bureaucracy at its disposal. What has the Left Guomindang? For the time being, nothing or almost nothing. The slogan of soviets is a call for the creation of real organs of the new state power right through the transitional régime of a dual government.

32) And what will be the attitude of the soviets to the "government of the revolutionary Guomindang", allegedly the "only" governmental authority "in this region"? A truly classic question! The attitude of the soviets to the revolutionary Guomindang will correspond to the attitude of the revolutionary Guomindang to the soviets. In other words: to the extent that the soviets arise, arm themselves, consolidate themselves, they will tolerate over them only such a government as bases itself upon the armed workers and peasants. What makes the soviet system valuable is the fact that, especially in directly revolutionary epochs, it furnishes the best means of guaranteeing agreement between the central and local government authorities.

33) Comrade Stalin, as far back as 1925, called the Guomindang a "workers' and peasants' party". This definition has nothing in common with Marxism. But it is clear that with this incorrect formulation comrade Stalin wanted to express the idea that the basis of the Guomindang is an anti-bourgeois alliance of the workers and peasants. This was absolutely false for the period in which it was said: the workers and peasants, it is true, did follow the Guomindang, but they were led by the bourgeoisie and we know where it led them.

Such a party is called bourgeois, and not workers' and peasants'. After the "withdrawal" of the bourgeoisie (that is, after it massacred the unarmed and unprepared proletariat), the revolution, according to Stalin, passes over to a new stage, in which it is to be led by the Left Guomindang, that is, by one, at least so we are to assume, that will finally realize the Stalinist idea of the "workers' and peasants' party". The question arises: why then will the creation of workers' and peasants' soviets mean a war against the authority of the workers' and peasants' Guomindang?

34) Another argument: To call for the creation of soviets "means to hand the enemies of the Chinese people a new weapon to combat the revolution, to manufacture new legends and to pretend that there is no national revolution in China, but an artificial transplanting of Moscow sovietization".

This stupefying argument means that if we develop, extend and deepen the revolutionary movement of the masses, the enemies of the Chinese people will redouble their efforts to calumniate it. This argument has no other sense. Therefore it has no sense at all.

Perhaps the theses have not in mind the enemies of the Chinese people, but the fear of the popular masses themselves of a Moscow sovietization? But on what is such a consideration based? It is well known that all the varieties of the "national" bourgeoisie, right, centre and left, zealously smear themselves with a protective Muscovite colouration in all their political work: they create commissars, political army posts, political departments, plenums of the central committee, control commissions, etc. The Chinese bourgeoisie is not at all afraid of transplanting Muscovite forms, which it carefully debases to serve its own class aims. But why do they apply them? Not out of love for Moscow, but rather because they are popular with the masses of the people. The Chinese peasant knows that the soviets gave the land to the Russian peasant, and whoever does not know this ought to learn it. The Chinese workers know that the soviets guaranteed the liberty of the Russian proletariat. The experience of the counter-revolution of Chiang Kai-shek must have made the advanced workers understand that without an independent organization embracing the whole proletariat and assuring its collaboration with the oppressed masses in the city and on the land, the revolution cannot triumph. The creation of soviets follows for the Chinese masses from their own experience, and is far from being an "artificially transplanted sovietization" for them. A policy that is afraid to call things by their right name is a false policy. One must be guided by the revolutionary masses and by the objective needs of the revolution, but not by what the enemy will say.

35) It is said: The Hankow government is nevertheless a fact. Feng Yuxiang is a fact, Tang Shengzhi is a fact, and they have armed forces at their disposal; neither the Wuhan government nor Feng Yuxiang, nor Tang Shengzhi wants soviets. To create soviets would mean to break with these allies. Although this argument is not openly formulated in the theses, it is nevertheless decisive for many comrades. We have already heard from Stalin on the Hankow government: the "revolutionary centre", the "only governmental authority". At the same time an advertising campaign is launched for

Feng Yuxiang in our party meetings: "a former worker", "a faithful revolutionist", "a reliable man", etc. All this is a repetition of the past mistakes under circumstances in which these mistakes can become even more disastrous. The Hankow government and the army command can be against the soviets only because they will have nothing to do with a radical agrarian program, with a real break with the large landowners and the bourgeoisie, because they secretly cherish the thought of a compromise with the right. But then it becomes all the more important to form soviets. This is the only way to push the revolutionary elements of Hankow to the left and force the counter-revolutionists to retire.

36) But even if the soviets do not carry on a war with the "only" government of Hankow, will they not still bring with them the elements of dual power? Without a doubt. Whoever is really for the course towards a workers' and peasants' government, not only in words but in deeds, must understand that this course leads through a certain period of dual power. How long this period will last, what concrete forms it will assume, will depend upon how the "only" government in Hankow conducts itself, upon the independence and initiative of the Communist Party, upon how rapidly the soviets develop, etc. It will be our task, in any case, to strengthen the element of the workers and peasants in the dual power and by that provide the genuine workers' and peasants' soviet government with a fully developed democratic program.

37) But dozens of foreign warships are anchored in the Yangtze river which can sweep away Shanghai,

Hankow, etc. Is it not insanity to form soviets under such conditions? This argument too is, of course, not formulated in Stalin's theses, but it is paraded around everywhere in Party meetings (Martynov, Yaroslavsky and others). The school of Martynov would like to kill the idea of the soviets with fear of the British naval artillery. This artifice is not a new one. In 1917, the Social Revolutionists and the Mensheviks sought to frighten us by declaring that the seizure of power by the soviets would mean the occupation of Kronstadt and Petrograd by the Allies. We answered: only the deepening of the revolution can save it. Foreign imperialism will only reconcile itself to such a "revolution" as strengthens its own positions in China at the price of a few concessions to the Chinese bourgeoisie. Every real people's revolution that undermines the colonial foundation of imperialism will inevitably meet with the latter's furious resistance. We did try to stop halfway, but this "only correct line" protected Nanking from the cannon of imperialism as little as it did the Chinese workers from the machine-guns of Chiang Kai-shek. Only the transition of the Chinese revolution to the phase of real mass action, only the formation of workers', peasants' and soldiers' soviets, only the deepening of the social program of the revolution, are capable, as our own experiences prove, of bringing confusion into the ranks of the foreign armed forces by arousing their sympathy for the soviets and thus really protecting the revolution from blows from without.

# What Do the Theses of Stalin Propose in Place of Soviets?

38) The creation of "revolutionary peasant committees, workers' trade unions, and other mass organizations as preparatory elements for the soviets of the future". What should be the course of these organizations? We do not find a single word on this in the theses. The phrase that these are "preparatory elements for the soviets of the future" is only a phrase and nothing more. What will these organizations do now? They will have to conduct strikes, boycotts, break the backbone of the bureaucratic apparatus, annihilate the counter-revolutionary military bands, drive out the large landowners, disarm the detachments of the usurers and the rich peasants, arm the workers and peasants, in a word, solve all the problems of the democratic and agrarian revolution that are on the order of the day, and in this way raise themselves to the position of local organs of power. But then they will be soviets, only of a kind that are badly suited to their tasks. The theses therefore propose, if these proposals are to be taken seriously at all, to create substitutes for soviets, instead of soviets themselves.

39) During all the preceding mass movements, the trade unions were compelled to fulfil functions closely approaching the functions of soviets (Hong Kong, Shanghai, and elsewhere). But these were precisely the functions for which the trade unions were entirely insufficient. They embrace a too small number of workers. They do not at all embrace the petty-bourgeois

masses in the city that incline towards the proletariat. But such tasks as the carrying through of strikes with the least possible losses to the poorer population of the city, the distribution of provisions, participation in tax policy, participation in the formation of armed forces, to say nothing of carrying through the agrarian revolution in the provinces, can be accomplished with the necessary sweep only when the directing organization embraces not only all the sections of the proletariat, but connects them intimately in the course of its activities with the poor population in the city and country. One would at least think that the military *coup d'état* of Chiang Kai-shek had finally hammered into the mind of every revolutionist the fact that trade unions separated from the army are one thing, and united workers' and soldiers' soviets, on the other hand, are quite another thing. Revolutionary trade unions and peasants' committees can arouse the hatred of the enemy no less than soviets. But they are far less capable than soviets of warding off its blows.

If we are to speak seriously of the alliance of the proletariat with the oppressed masses in the city and country – not of an "alliance" between the leaders, a semi-adulterated alliance through dubious representatives, but of a real fighting alliance built and steeled in the struggles of the masses against the enemy – then such an alliance can have no other organizational form than that of soviets. This can be denied only by those who rely more upon compromising leaders than upon the revolutionary masses below.

# Should We Break with the Left Guomindang?

From the foregoing remarks may be seen how ill-founded are the whispers about a break of the Communist Party with the Guomindang. "This is tantamount," say the theses, "to deserting the field of struggle and leaving our allies in the Guomindang in the lurch to the delight of the enemies of the revolution." These pathetic lines are quite out of place. It is not a question of a break but of preparing a bloc, not on the basis of subordination but on the basis of a genuine equality of rights. A revolutionary Guomindang has yet to be formed. We are in favour of the Communists working inside the Guomindang and patiently drawing the workers and peasants over to their side. The Communist Party can gain a petty-bourgeois ally, not by prostrating itself before the Guomindang at every one of its vacillations, but only if it appeals to the workers openly and directly, in its own name, under its own banner, organizes them around it and shows the Guomindang by example and by deed what a party of the masses is, by supporting every forward step of the Guomindang, by relentlessly unmasking every vacillation, every step backward, and by creating a real revolutionary foundation for a bloc with the Guomindang in the form of workers', peasants' and soldiers' soviets.

40) It is absurd to assert that the Opposition stands for the "political isolation" of the Communist Party. This assertion contains just as much truth as the one that the Opposition stood for withdrawing from the

British trade unions. Both accusations have only served to mask the bloc with the right Guomindang and with the traitorous General Council. The Opposition is energetically in favour of strengthening and developing the bloc with the revolutionary elements of the Guomindang, for a compact fighting alliance of the workers with the poor population of the city and country, for the course towards the revolutionary dictatorship of the workers, peasants and the urban petty-bourgeoisie.

For this it is necessary:

a. to recognize as disastrous such forms of the bloc in which the Communist Party sacrifices the interests of the workers and peasants to the utopian aim of holding the bourgeoisie in the camp of the national revolution;
b. to reject categorically such forms of the bloc in which the Communist Party hauls down its banner and sacrifices the growth of its own influence and its own authority in the interest of its allies;
c. to approve a bloc with clearly formulated common tasks, but not to base it upon misunderstanding, diplomatic manoeuvres, sycophancy and hypocrisy;
d. to lay down the conditions and limits of the bloc with thorough precision and let them be known to all;
e. for the Communist Party to retain full freedom of criticism, and to watch over its allies with no less vigilance than over an enemy, without forgetting for a moment that an ally who bases himself upon other classes or depends upon other classes is only a

      temporary confederate who can be transformed by the force of circumstances into an opponent and an enemy;
f. to set the connection with the petty-bourgeois masses higher than a connection with their party leaders;
g. finally, to rely only upon ourselves, upon our own organization, arms and power.

Only by observing these conditions will a really revolutionary bloc of the Communist Party with the Guomindang become possible, not a bloc of the leaders, which vacillates and is subject to contingencies, but a bloc based upon all the oppressed masses of the city and country under the political hegemony of the proletarian vanguard.

# The Problems of the Chinese Revolution and the Anglo-Russian Committee

41) In the direction of the Chinese revolution we are confronted not by tactical errors, but by a radically false line. This follows clearly from everything that has been presented above. It becomes still clearer when the policy in China is compared with our policy towards the Anglo-Russian Committee. In the latter case the inconsistency of the opportunistic line did not express itself so tragically as in China, but no less completely and convincingly.

42) In England, as in China, the line was directed towards a rapprochement with the "solid" leaders, based on personal relations, on diplomatic combinations, while renouncing in practice the deepening of the abyss between the revolutionary or leftward-developing masses and the traitorous leaders. We ran after Chiang Kai-shek and thereby drove the Chinese Communists to accept the dictatorial conditions put by Chiang Kai-shek to the Communist Party. In so far as the representatives of the All-Russian Central Council of Trade Unions ran after Purcell, Hicks, Citrine and Company and adopted in principle the position of neutrality in the trade-union movement, they recognized the General Council as the only representative of the British proletariat and obligated themselves not to interfere in the affairs of the British labour movement.

43) The decisions of the Berlin Conference of the Anglo-Russian Committee mean our renunciation of support in the future to strikers against the will of avowed

strikebreakers. They are tantamount to a condemnation and a flat betrayal of the trade-union minority, all of whose activity is directed against the traitors whom we have recognized as the sole representatives of the English working class. Finally, the solemn proclamation of "non-interference" signifies our capitulation in principle to the national narrowness of the labour movement in its most backward and most conservative form.

44) Chiang Kai-shek accuses us of interfering in the internal affairs of China just as Citrine accuses us of interfering in the internal affairs of the trade unions. Both accusations are only transcriptions of the accusation of world imperialism against a workers' state which dares to interest itself in the fate of the oppressed masses of the whole world. In this case as in others, Chiang Kai-shek, like Citrine, under different conditions and at different posts, remain the agents of imperialism despite temporary conflicts with it. If we chase after collaboration with such "leaders", we are forced ever more to restrict, to limit and to emasculate our methods of revolutionary mobilization.

45) Through our false policy we not only helped the General Council to maintain its tottering positions after the strike betrayal, but, what is more, we furnished it with all the necessary weapons for putting impudent demands to us which we meekly accepted. Under the tinkling of phrases about "hegemony", we acted in the Chinese revolution and the British labour movement as if we were morally vanquished, and by that we prepared our material defeat. An opportunist deviation is always accompanied by a loss of faith in one's own line.

46) The businessmen of the General Council, having received a guarantee of non-interference from the All-Russian Central Council of Trade Unions, are undoubtedly persuading Chamberlain that their method of struggle against Bolshevik propaganda is far more effective than ultimatums and threats. Chamberlain, however, prefers the combined method and combines the diplomacy of the General Council with the violence of British imperialism.

47) If it is alleged against the Opposition that Baldwin or Chamberlain "also" wants the dissolution of the Anglo-Russian Committee, then one understands nothing at all of the political mechanics of the bourgeoisie. Baldwin justly feared and still fears the harmful influence of the Soviet trade unions upon the leftward-developing labour movement of Britain. The British bourgeoisie set its pressure upon the General Council against the pressure of the All-Russian Central Council of Trade Unions upon the traitorous leaders of the trade unions, and on this field the bourgeoisie triumphed all along the line. The General Council refused to accept money from the Soviet trade unions and to confer with them on the question of aid for the mine workers. In exercising its pressure upon the General Council, the British bourgeoisie, through it, exerted pressure upon the All-Russian Central Council of Trade Unions and at the Berlin Conference obtained from the latter's representatives an unprecedented capitulation on the fundamental questions of the class struggle. An Anglo-Russian Committee *of this kind* only serves the British bourgeoisie (cf. the declaration

of **The Times**). This will not hinder it from continuing its pressure in the future upon the General Council, and demanding of it a break with the All-Russian Central Council of Trade Unions, for by such a policy of pressure and blackmail the British bourgeoisie wins everything we lose by our senseless and unprincipled conduct.

48) The insinuations that Chiang Kai-shek is "in solidarity" with the Opposition, because he wants to drive the Communists out of the Guomindang, have the same value. A remark by Chiang Kai-shek is being circulated in which he is supposed to have said to another general that he agrees with the Opposition in the CPSU on this point. In the text of the document from which this "quotation" was picked out, the words of Chiang Kai-shek are not adduced as an expression of his views, but as a manifestation of his readiness and aptitude to deceit, to falsehood, and even to disguise himself for a few days as a "Left Communist" in order to be better able to stab us in the back. Still more, the document in question is one long indictment against the line and the work of the Comintern's representatives in China. Instead of picking quotations out of the document and giving them a sense contrary to that contained in the text, it would be better to make the document itself known to the Comintern. Leave aside, however, the misuse of alleged "quotations" and there remains the "coincidence" that Chiang Kai-shek has always been against a bloc with the Communists, while we are against a bloc with Chiang Kai-shek. The school of Martynov draws from this the conclusion that the policy of the Opposition "generally" serves the

reaction. This accusation is not new either. The whole development of Bolshevism in Russia proceeded under the accompaniment of Menshevik accusations that the Bolsheviks were playing the game of the reaction, that they were aiding the monarchy against the Kadets, the Kadets against the SRs and Mensheviks, and so on without end. Renaudel accuses the French Communists of rendering aid to Poincaré when they attack the bloc of the radicals and the Socialists. The German Social Democrats have more than once pretended that our refusal to enter the League of Nations plays the game of the extreme imperialists, etc., etc.

The fact that the big bourgeoisie, represented by Chiang Kai-shek, needs to break with the proletariat, and the revolutionary proletariat on the other hand needs to break with bourgeoisie, is not an evidence of their solidarity, but of the irreconcilable class antagonism between them. The hopeless compromisers stand between the bourgeoisie and the proletariat and accuse both the "extreme" wings of disrupting the national front and rendering assistance to the reaction. To accuse the Opposition of playing the game of Chamberlain, Thomas or Chiang Kai-shek is to show a narrow-minded opportunism, and at the same time to recognize involuntarily the proletarian and revolutionary character of our political line.

49) The Berlin Conference of the Anglo-Russian Committee which coincided with the beginning of British intervention in China, did not even dare to allude to the question of effective measures to take against the hangman's work of British imperialism in the Far East. Could a more striking proof be found that the

Anglo-Russian Committee is incapable of moving as much as a finger towards really preventing war? But it is not simply useless. It has brought immeasurable harm to the revolutionary movement, like every illusion and hypocrisy. By referring to its collaboration with the All-Russian Central Council of Trade Unions in the "struggle for peace", the General Council is able to soothe and lull the consciousness of the British proletariat, stirred by the danger of war. The All-Russian Central Council of Trade Unions now appears before the British working class and the working class of the whole world as a sort of guarantor for the international policy of the traitors of the General Council. The criticism directed by the revolutionary elements in Britain against the General Council thereby becomes weakened and blunted. Thanks to Purcell, Hicks and Company, the MacDonalds and Thomases get the possibility of keeping the working masses in a stupor up to the threshold of war itself, in order to call upon them then for the defence of the democratic fatherland. When comrade Tomsky, in his last interview (**Pravda**, May 8), criticized the Thomases, Havelock Wilsons and the other hirelings of the Stock Exchange, he did not mention by a single word the subversive, disintegrating, lulling, and therefore much more pernicious work of Purcell, Hicks and Company. These "allies" are not mentioned by name in the interview as though they do not even exist. Then why a bloc with them? But they do exist. Without them Thomas does not exist politically. Without Thomas there exists no Baldwin, that is, the capitalist régime in England. Contrary to our best intentions, our support of the bloc with Purcell is actually support of the whole British régime and the facilitation of its work in China. After all that has happened, this is clear to every revolutionist who has gone through the school of Lenin. In a like manner, our collaboration with Chiang Kai-shek blunted the class vigilance of the Chinese proletariat, and thereby facilitated the April *coup d'état.*

# The Theory of Stages and the Theory of Socialism in One Country

50) The *chvostist* theory of "stages" or "steps" repeatedly proclaimed by Stalin in recent times, has served as the motivation in principle for the opportunist tactic. If the complete organizational and political independence of the Chinese Communist Party is demanded, it means that steps are being skipped over. If soviet organizations are demanded for drawing the worker and peasant masses into the civil war, it means that "stages" are being skipped over. If the dissolution of the political bloc with the traitors of the General Council, who are now carrying on the basest work, is demanded, it means that stages are being skipped over. The conservative bourgeois-national Guomindang government, the military command of Chiang Kai-shek, the General Council – in a word, any one of the institutions created by the pressure of the possessing and ruling classes, and constituting a barrier for the revolutionary class movement, becomes, according to this theory, a great historical stage, to which one's policy must be adapted until "the masses themselves" pass through it. Once we set out on this road, our policy must be inevitably transformed from a revolutionary factor into a conservative one. The course of the Chinese revolution and the fate of the Anglo-Russian Committee are an imminent warning in this regard.

51) Such facts as the defeat of the great strikes of the British proletariat last year, as the Chinese revolution this year, cannot go by without consequences for the

international labour movement, just as the defeat of the German proletariat in the autumn of 1923 did not pass without leaving its traces. An unavoidable temporary weakening of the revolutionary positions is in itself a great evil. It can become irreparable for a long time if the orientation is wrong, if the strategic line is false. Precisely now, in the period of a temporary revolutionary ebb, the struggle against all manifestations of opportunism and national limitedness and for the line of revolutionary internationalism is more necessary than ever.

By recognizing the principle of non-interference, our delegation, regardless of its intentions, promotes the most conservative, most defeatist tendencies in the working class. There is nothing perplexing in the fact that the most backward and weariest sections of the workers of the USSR consider interference in the British strike struggle or the Chinese revolution a mistake. Ever more frequently they argue: "Are we not taught that we can build up socialism in our country, even without the victory of the revolution in other countries, if only there no intervention? Then we must carry on such a policy as does not provoke intervention. Our interference in British and Chinese affairs is a mistake, because without yielding positive results it drives the world bourgeoisie on to the road of military intervention and thus threatens the construction of socialism in our country."

There is no doubt and there can be none that now, after the new defeats of the international revolutionary movement, the theory of socialism in one country will serve, independent of the will of its creators, to justify, to motivate and to sanctify all the tendencies directed towards restricting the revolutionary objectives, towards quenching the ardour of the struggle, towards a national and conservative narrowness.

The slightest digression towards the side of "non-interference", whether covered or not with the theory of socialism in one country, only increases the imperialist danger instead of diminishing it.

It is perfectly clear and incontestable with regard to the Chinese revolution that only a deeper mass impulsion, a more radical social program, the slogan of the workers' and peasants' soviets, can seriously shield the revolution from a military attack from without. Only a revolution on whose banner the toilers and oppressed write plainly their own demands is capable of gripping the feelings not only of the international proletariat but also of the soldiers of capital. We know this well enough from our own experiences. We saw and proved it in the years of the civil war at Archangel, Odessa and elsewhere. The compromising and traitorous leadership did not protect Nanking from destruction. It facilitated the penetration of the enemy ships into the Yangtze. A revolutionary leadership, with a powerful social movement, can make the waters of the Yangtze too hot for the ships of Lloyd George, Chamberlain and MacDonald. In any case, this is the only way and the only hope of defence.

The extension of the soviet front is simultaneously the best defence of the USSR. Under the present circumstances, the talk that our international position has become worse, or can in any way become worse, as a result of some kind of "left" mistake, sounds absurd. If our position has grown worse, it is a result of the defeat of the Chinese revolution, a historical and international event, regardless of whether or not we interfere in it. Were we not to interfere in the intervention of imperialism, we would only facilitate its work – against China, and against ourselves as well. But there is a difference between interference and interference. The falsest and most dangerous interference consists of the endeavour to halt the development of the revolution half-way. The struggle for peace occupies the centre of our international policy. But even the most extreme representative of the Martynov school would never dare to contend that our policy of peace can be in contradiction to the development of the Chinese revolution, or inversely, that its development can be in contradiction to our policy of peace. The one supplements the other. The best way to defend the USSR is to vanquish the Chiang Kai-shek counter-revolution and to raise the movement to a higher stage. Whoever rejects soviets for China under such conditions, disarms the Chinese revolution. Whoever proclaims the principle of non-interference in the relations of the European proletariat weakens its revolutionary vanguard. Both weaken the position of the USSR, the principal fortress of the international proletariat.

Thus we see how one mistake is heaped upon the others and together produce a line which digresses ever more from the line of Bolshevism. Critical voices and warnings are regarded as obstructions. The shifting of the official line towards the right is supplemented by blows at the left. To continue on this path would involve the greatest dangers for the soviet state as well as for the Comintern. Were we to conceal these dangers from the international proletarian vanguard, we would be betraying the banner of Communism.

\* \* \*

We do not doubt for a moment that the mistakes can be repaired, the deviations overcome, and the line rectified without violent crises and convulsions. The language of facts is all too eloquent, the lessons of experience all too plain. It is only necessary that our party, of the Soviet Union as well as of the International, obtains the full possibility to weigh the facts and draw the proper conclusions from them. We firmly believe that they will draw these conclusions in the spirit of revolutionary unity.

# Notes

1. The theses of Comrade Stalin are published in the name of the Central Committee. This does not change the fact that the theses were not examined by the plenum of the Central Committee. The Political Committee charged three members, Comrades Stalin, Bukharin and Molotov, to look over the theses of Comrade Stalin and, in case of agreement, to publish them in the name of the Central Committee. Naturally, it is not a question of the formal side of the matter, which nobody raises. But it is quite clear that such a "simplified" method of deciding questions of world importance, after the mistakes made and the heavy defeats, in no way serves the interests of the party and of the Chinese revolution. – L.T.

2. *First Letter from Afar*, Lenin, Vol.XIV, part 1, pp.10-11; **Pravda**, March 21, 1917.

3. No.8, April 23, 1927, p.4.

4. **Sotsialisticheski Vestnik**, April 23, 1927, p.3.

5. **Pravda**, April 23, 1927.

6. Raskolnikov's foreword to the pamphlet by Tang Pingshan.

7. **Problems of Leninism**, page 264.